338.4

Real

ES

THE MOTOR INDUSTRY

REAL LIFE GUIDES

Practical guides for practical people

In this increasingly sophisticated world the need for manually skilled people to build our homes, cut our hair, fix our boilers and make our cars go is greater than ever. As things progress, so the level of training and competence required of our skilled manual workers increases.

In this series of career guides from Trotman, we look in detail at what it takes to train for, get into and be successful at a wide spectrum of practical careers. *Real Life Guides* aim to inform and inspire young people and adults alike by providing comprehensive yet hard-hitting and often blunt information about what it takes to succeed in these areas.

The other titles in the series are:

Real Life Guide: The Armed Forces
Real Life Guide: The Beauty Industry
Real Life Guide: Care
Real Life Guide: Carpentry and Cabinet-Making
Real Life Guide: Catering
Real Life Guide: Construction
Real Life Guide: Distribution and Logistics
Real Life Guide: Electrician
Real Life Guide: The Fire Service
Real Life Guide: Hairdressing
Real Life Guide: Plumbing
Real Life Guide: The Police Force
Real Life Guide: Retailing
Real Life Guide: Transport
Real Life Guide: Working Outdoors
Real Life Guide: Working with Animals and Wildlife
Real Life Guide: Working with Young People

trotman

Real Life

GUIDES

THE MOTOR INDUSTRY

Dee Pilgrim
Second edition

Real Life Guide to The Motor Industry
This second edition published in 2007 by Trotman, an imprint of
Crimson Publishing, Westminster House, Kew Road, Richmond,
Surrey TW9 2ND
www.crimsonpublishing.co.uk

© Trotman 2007

First edition written by Mike Hobbs, published 2004
by Trotman and Co Ltd
Reprinted 2005

Editorial and Publishing Team
Author Dee Pilgrim
Editorial Mina Patria, Publishing Director; Jo Jacomb,
Managing Editor;
Production John
Sales and Marke
Advertising Sarah

Designed by XAB

Trotman gratefully
Automotive Skills i

British Library Cataloguing in Publications Data
A catalogue record for this book is available from the British
Library

ISBN 978 1 84455 119 4

Typeset by Photoprint, Torquay
Printed and bound in Great Britain by
Creative Print & Design, Wales

GUIDES

CONTENTS

About the author

Dee Pilgrim completed the pre-entry, periodical journalism course at the London College of Printing before working on a variety of music and women's titles. She has written numerous articles and interviews for *Company*, *Cosmopolitan*, *New Woman*, *Woman's Journal* and *Weight Watchers* magazines. For many years she covered new output by singer/songwriters for *Top* magazine, which was distributed via Tower Records stores, and during this period interviewed the likes of Tori Amos, Tom Robinson and Joan Armatrading. As a freelancer for Independent Magazines she concentrated on celebrity interviews and film, theatre and restaurant reviews for magazines such as *Ms London*, *Girl About Town*, *LAM* and *Nine to Five*, and in her capacity as a critic she has appeared on both radio and television. She is currently the film reviewer for *Now* magazine and has written a number of titles for Trotman. When not attending film screenings she is active in the Critics' Circle and is the secretary for its film section.

Foreword

Looking for a career that combines your love of cars with the opportunity for early management or to run your own business, then a career in the automotive industry could be for you. The automotive industry employs over half a million people across the UK and of course it is a global skill, in demand internationally.

In such a large industry it is pretty certain that there will be a job for you, be it working as a fast fit technician in a tyre or brake centre, helping people at the roadside when their car breaks down, maintaining and repairing vehicles in a dealership or garage or specialising in specific systems (air conditioning and alarm systems for example) or 'pimping wheels' through body repair and painting.

Practical and problem solving skills are obviously important but you will also need the ability to understand customer needs and to apply maths and science. Increasingly, technicians need to be able to use diagnostic equipment in the course of their day.

You may be able to get your first experience at school, through a City & Guilds entry qualification in motor vehicles but the serious training starts when you start your apprenticeship. On the apprenticeship you will combine learning within a college or private training body with practical skills gained in the workplace. Throughout the course flexibility is key with different pathways available for whatever field or aspect you choose, be it motor cycles, cars, trucks or buses. It's worth mentioning that the big manufacturers such as Honda run their own apprenticeship programmes that you can apply to directly.

City & Guilds are delighted to be part of the Trotman *Real Life Guides* series to help raise your awareness of these vocational qualifications. Further information and advice on the range of careers available is available free from the Sector Skills Council for the automotive industry, Automotive Skills (www.automotiveskills.org.uk) or by calling their careers hotline on 0800 093 1777.

Graham Goodwin
Automotive Manager
City & Guilds

Introduction

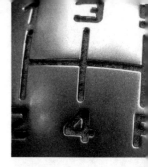

The British public's love affair with the automobile has been a long and distinguished one. Although we may not favour the gas-guzzling monsters that are so close to the hearts of Americans, we are still fiercely attached to our motorcars, so much so that the proportion of vehicles to people in the UK is at least as high as it is in the USA. Incredibly, the annual turnover of our motor industry is in the region of £180 billion. It directly employs 584,000 people in 69,000 businesses and overall the industry supports over 1.9 million jobs, that's 6.4 per cent of the entire UK workforce.

While environmentalists may rage about congestion, toxic fumes and the dangers of building even more motorways, the truth is that the motorcar is not going to go away. We need lorries and tankers to carry goods around the country – everything from oil and milk to medicines, food and electrical goods – while many of us simply could not get to work or school without the use of either the private family car or the local bus.

Many of us simply could not get to work or school without the use of either the private family car or the local bus

Just think about an ordinary family on any ordinary day. After the school run, mum or dad may use the car to get to work. If mum has a job as a travelling pharmaceuticals representative, then she'll be using the car to visit clients. After work dad may drive to the local sports centre to play a game of squash, or he may go to the supermarket to stock up on groceries, or the whole family may take a trip to the local cinema.

For whatever reasons different people use their cars, the very fact that so many of us own one means there are huge numbers of them to produce, assemble, sell and maintain. And that is not just true of cars for private ownership either. Someone has to make and maintain local transport buses, as well as taxis and other public use vehicles such as fire engines, ambulances and police vans – and don't forget the two-wheeled variety of vehicles that also use our roads.

Although the days of the UK being one of the world's leading motor vehicle manufacturers may be over, there is still a surprisingly respectable core of people employed in assembly and production. But their number is still relatively modest compared with those who are employed in the motor industry in servicing, maintaining, repairing and selling vehicles. According to the Office of National Statistics (ONS), in 2004 there were 195,983 motor technicians/automotive engineers working in Britain alongside 30,280 vehicle body builders and repairers, and 18,262 vehicle spray painters.

The number of jobs in this service branch of the trade is spread fairly evenly throughout the UK, so that is the area on which this book will concentrate, rather than the manufacturing work that is necessarily based around the production centres.

This book is not trying to be an in-depth guide to all the different parts of the motor industry, but it will give you an overview of the various jobs available to help you decide whether one of them is right for you. You'll learn about the work involved through case studies, examples of a typical working day, job rundowns and quotes so that you can put together a mental picture of life in every aspect of the motor trade.

Your attitude and relevant skills will be tested by a series of quizzes, and you will be able to question your own values to see whether they match those encountered in the industry. In short, you will gain every possible insight into the world of vehicles to determine whether it's the career for you.

Although the days of the UK being one of the world's leading motor vehicle manufacturers may be over, there is still a surprisingly respectable core of people employed in assembly and production

You will also be able to find out where you can go on training courses, get some work experience or have the best chance to nail that elusive first job. If this book doesn't tell you precisely what you need to know about a particular aspect of the industry (and it's a bigger subject than any single book could possibly contain), then one of the links to websites and further information is sure to point you in the right direction.

If you're about to leave school or college and are interested in finding out what the motor industry holds in store, then this book is for you. You'll also find hints and suggestions about preparing CVs and PDPs (personal development plans) to present yourself in the best manner to potential employers. It will also be useful if you're stuck in a job that has lost its appeal and are considering changing your career before it's too late.

Whether you are a car fanatic or not particularly interested in what goes on inside an internal combustion engine, this book will help you to determine whether there is a place for you within Britain's thriving motor industry. If you are interested in the driving side of things and want to be the country's next Jensen Button, if you dream of designing a car as successful as the beloved Mini, or if you simply want to sell them, this book will help you to green light your career and to achieve your future aims.

LEWIS HAMILTON

Success story

THE FORMULA ONE DRIVER
*Born in Stevenage in 1985, 22-year-old
Lewis Hamilton is the first black driver ever
to make it to Formula One.*

He started his driving career when his dad
bought him a radio-controlled car when he
was five years old. When he was seven he
progressed to a go-kart and he won the
Cadet Class of the British National Karting
Championship three years later. Then,
when he was just 12 years old, he became
involved with the McLaren and Mercedes-
Benz Young Driver Support Programme.
The programme was set up in 1998 to
provide a structured environment for
nurturing and developing future driver
talent. As well as providing financial and
technical backing, the programme provides
professional advice to up and coming
racing drivers.

Lewis dominated the 2003 British Formula
Renault Championship winning 10 out of
the Championship's 15 races and was
presented with a British Racing Drivers'
Club (BRDC) 'Rising Star' Trophy, and won
the *Autosport* Club Driver of the Year
award in the same year. In 2004 Lewis

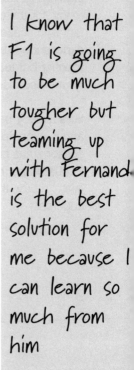

I know that
F1 is going
to be much
tougher but
teaming up
with Fernand.
is the best
solution for
me because I
can learn so
much from
him

competed in the prominent Formula 3 Euro Series with Manor Motorsport, then in 2005 he dominated the F3 Euro Series Championship, being crowned champion in August with four rounds of the series still to be contested. He had an unbeatable 48-point lead over his closest rival, having taken 11 victories, 10 pole positions and 13 podiums. In 2006, after becoming the GP2 Series Champion, he reached the pinnacle of racing driving when he was named as Fernando Alonso's new McLaren Formula One team-mate, starting his first F1 season in 2007. He says he's 'absolutely ready' for the challenge. 'I have nothing left to prove. I had a fantastic season winning the GP2 Series against some very experienced drivers. I know that F1 is going to be much tougher but teaming up with Fernando is the best solution for me because I can learn so much from him.'

He's already been dubbed the Tiger Woods of motorsport and is expected to earn about £350,000 in his first F1 season, plus bonuses that could amount to as much as £140,000 per race. He already has his eyes on a suitably flashy motor, the extra special Mercedes SLR McLaren supercar.

What's the story?

The motor industry brings a lot of money into the UK economy, creates a lot of jobs and helps our import/export balance. But it is valuable in other ways too.

The continuing vibrancy of our motor industry ensures that old skills don't die out and new skills are added all the time. This broadening of the skills base is vital for maintaining Britain's market share of the industry. If our skills fall behind those in the rest of the world, we will lose business to other countries.

Dominic Luddy is the Sector Careers Manager for Automotive Skills, the Sector Skills Council for the motor industry, he says: 'We have to ensure the training providers are up to speed with the industry because it changes so rapidly. For instance, a car built just five years ago is very different from a car built today. Twenty years ago the jobs in automotive construction and repair would have been very mechanically orientated, but now they are very technology specific and we are now trying to get across a white coat image rather than a greasy garage (image). This is the way the industry is going; we don't use the term mechanic anymore, we call them technicians. Although we do need people with all levels of ability, because technology is advancing so fast we need people who have management level potential and who have an interest in technology, who can do diagnostic work using the sophisticated systems that are now in place.'

In fact, at present there is a lack of skilled workers coming through the system and this is happening for a variety of reasons. For a start, the industry has a problem recruiting both females and ethnic minority workers. 'It would be desirable to have 50 per cent of the workforce female,' says Dominic. 'The latest statistics show around only 1.5 per cent of trainees on motor vehicle tecnician courses are female. It's exceptionally poor but we are addressing this issue.' Another reason is that the industry is not attracting the graduates and higher qualified recruits it now needs. 'It's difficult because so many industries are crying out for Level 3 skills so we are all chasing the same candidates, which means we are suffering from a lack of skilled workers,' explains Dominic. Another upshot of this is that the average age of motor technicians working in the industry has now risen to 33 years. Basically, the industry is crying out for new blood, but if you were to join this vibrant, fast moving sector, what could you do?

All work in the motor industry can be divided into four main areas: designing and making vehicles, selling them, repairing and monitoring them and running a business.

DESIGNING AND MAKING VEHICLES
If you're interested in vehicle and engine technology, if you have the right academic qualifications and if you want to push the envelope by designing and producing really advanced machines for the new age, then the jobs in engineering are the ones to go for. Obviously they demand

expertise – it's not possible for just anyone to design and build a vehicle from scratch – but one of these may be the position you want to aim for in the future.

THE ENGINEERING JOBS
There are essentially six types of engineer in the motor industry.

1. The **Design Engineer** is the person who comes up with the original plans for the vehicle.

You have to be a visionary and be highly creative, yet you'll probably have evolved a strong practical streak too, based on learning what works and what doesn't, and knowing what's been successful in the past. However, you'll need to be willing to think outside the box and apply new technological ideas, and you'll have plenty of experience to back up your ideas.

You'll need to be willing to think outside the box and apply new technological ideas

2. Once the Design Engineer has provided a working blueprint, it's up to the **Development Engineer** to check that the plans are going to work in practice.

The balance in this job tips away slightly from the creative side towards the practical side, although you'll still be expected to suggest design improvements once you've translated the plans into something tangible and built the prototype. Essentially, Design and Development Engineers have to work together as a team.

3. Next, it's over to the **Production Engineer** to make sure that all the parts for the prototype vehicle are made and in proper functioning order.

This is the third job in the holy trinity of vehicle design, as it is essential to make sure that what is going to work as a prototype will also work consistently well for a production line vehicle, ensuring high quality control throughout.

4. The chief supporting job to these three is that of **Technician Engineer**, who often has to develop new machinery and equipment so that design testing and consequent manufacture can proceed according to plan.

You'll invariably pick up quite a lot of knowledge about all the different aspects of design, development and production. This can make technician engineers prime candidates for senior engineering roles.

5. When it comes to selling large quantities of vehicles, particularly overseas, the sales teams often need expert technical support. This is the main purpose of the **Sales Engineer**.

You'll have to combine in-depth engineering know-how with the ability to construct a convincing sales story (and often be fluent in foreign languages to communicate this). Only a few people possess such diverse skills to the necessary level.

6. Before tackling one of these five key tasks, most people who have gained their engineering degree are given the opportunity to become a **Graduate Engineer**, usually to

learn a little bit about the various aspects of each engineering role.

So, this is rather like an advanced trainee job, although the learning curve is fairly steep with correspondingly good promotion prospects.

OTHER MANUFACTURING JOBS

Once the senior engineering team has confirmed the detail of the plans, the principles of mass manufacturing take over and the job of building the vehicles passes to the production and assembly lines. Alternatively, the design-and-build process may have been done already, in which case vehicles will arrive in pre-produced pieces ready for assembly.

There are several skilled jobs in the manufacturing process.

1. The **Fitter/Mechanic/Technician** has the task of making sure that all the vehicle's mechanical parts are in proper working order. This is obviously a vital factor in proper systems of quality control.

2. Much of the assembly and production work in today's motor industry is controlled by computers and carried out by robots. The function of the **Tool Setter** is to adjust the computerised settings to reflect the different robotic techniques needed for any particular vehicle's manufacture.

3. Each vehicle has a multitude of different components. The **Pattern Maker** uses a variety of different materials to make castings that provide the correct patterns for each of these parts.

4. In building new vehicles, the **Body Builder** is at the heart of the construction process. Usually you'll work to fully detailed engineering plans, although sometimes (say, in the case of customised vehicles) you might create your own plans to provide a customer with a unique product.

Much of the assembly and production work in today's motor industry is controlled by computers and carried out by robots

5. It is the role of the **Craftsman** or **Craftswoman** to work on all aspects apart from the vehicle body to turn the engineering plans into reality. If you prove to be highly skilled and motivated by this job, it could be a stepping stone to engineering work, though that will require undertaking a full study programme.

6. Meanwhile, the **Body Maker** will be producing the sheet metal parts that enable the Body Builder to put together the finished article. You'll work to clear instructions in the case of both prototype and showroom models.

7. There is a great deal of electrical equipment involved in the manufacturing process and the **Electrician** has to make sure that it all functions smoothly and efficiently. At the same time, they have to check the quality control of electrical fittings in all the vehicles produced.

8. You can start training to do any of these jobs by becoming a **Trainee**, which will involve three or four years of study while continuing your day-to-day work.

SELLING MOTOR VEHICLES

In order for anything to be sold, potential customers first have to be aware of the product a manufacturer wants to sell. The process of attracting customers is called marketing and there are specialist jobs in this area of the industry.

Here is a quick guide to the seven that are most common.

1. If you want to make your way in sales, you will almost definitely have to start as a **Vehicle Sales Executive**. This is where you learn your trade, finding out what the customer wants and then identifying and offering a suitable vehicle from your portfolio of products. An effective sales executive needs all sorts of skills but the essential ones are the ability to communicate well, to listen carefully and to be knowledgeably enthusiastic.

2. After some time as a sales executive, if you show management potential, you may be given a spell as a **Sales Assistant**. This job has a dual purpose in that it allows you to provide complete back-up for the sales manager at the same time as it prepares you for a future in management.

It is possible to go straight into this job, but if you want to progress to management positions, some time involved in selling itself is a definite must.

3. Sooner or later, you'll get your chance to become a **Sales Manager**. This is where you'll learn how tricky it can be to manage a group of people, not least when they are all driven by ambition. You'll need to discover ways of inspiring your team and keeping them motivated while you make sure their expectations are realistic.

4. Eventually, when you've learned the complex art of team management, you can aspire to become a **Sales Director**. In some ways, this is just a larger version of a Sales Manager job, but you'll be expected to broaden your horizons and consider all the other factors that relate to the needs of the business as well as being concerned with sales.

The paradox for sales people is that, the more successful they are at sales and climb the promotion ladder, the less selling they have to do.

5. If you want to go into marketing management, you'll have to spend some time learning the basics as a **Marketing Assistant**. This position is often given to successful sales people to help them broaden their experience. Again, you'll be expected to support your boss, the Marketing Manager, in every part of the job while picking up great first-hand experience.

6. The job of the **Marketing Manager** is to broaden the potential customer base to its maximum extent and to ensure that the main advertising and promotional campaigns are aimed at those most likely to buy. You'll also have to demonstrate a great deal of general industry knowledge and learn what the opposition is doing right (and wrong).

7. Your ultimate aim is to become a **Marketing Director**. Often, the roles of Marketing Director and Sales Director are combined at board level. You'll have overall control of advertising and public relations, two specialist functions that are often contracted out to service organisations.

REPAIRING AND MAINTAINING MOTOR VEHICLES

The majority of people employed in the motor industry in the UK are involved either in maintaining or repairing vehicles, so the chances are that you'll go for a job in one of these areas. The standard garage jobs in this field are all technical roles.

1. Most people who enter this sector of the industry start off as a **Trainee Vehicle Technician**. This provides a good grounding in finding out what makes all types of vehicle tick.

2. You may want to specialise after a while and become a **Light Vehicle Technician** which, as the name suggests, means you would dedicate yourself solely to cars and light vans.

Maintenance is a high priority for motor vehicles because of the amount of wear and tear they sustain

3. A **Heavy Vehicle Technician** has a similar responsibility for maintaining and repairing lorries, coaches, buses and large vans.

4. If you have your own motorbike, it's more than likely you've spent a good deal of time tinkering with it, which would give you the right sort of background to be a **Motorcycle Technician**.

5. Every vehicle is crammed full of electrical equipment and it's the task of the **Auto Electrician** to make sure that all repairs and maintenance are carried out effectively.

Naturally, it's not just the engines or electrical systems that need maintenance and repair. The bodywork can also be damaged and need repairing, as can other materials in the vehicle. The following are the main jobs that come up in these areas.

1. Like its counterpart in the manufacturing process, the job of **Body Fitter** is fixing together body panels, the only difference being that this time all the damaged parts of the bodywork have to be removed before they can be reassembled.

2. The **Body Finisher** is mainly concerned with paintwork, respraying the vehicle body until it is restored and looks as good as new. Applying a paint finish is not confined to repaired vehicles, though – it applies to customised ones as well.

3. As you would expect, the **Body Repairer** has the task of making repairs or alterations to the bodywork. In such cases, the vehicle does not need to be completely refitted but needs partial replacement or repair.

4. When they've been repaired or had modifications done to them, all vehicles need to look spruce both inside and out. The job of the **Valeter** is to clean all interiors and exteriors (and the engine if necessary) to ensure that everything is in good working order. Often you'll find yourself doing this to help prepare vehicles for sale.

5. There's a lot of glass in most motor vehicles and, as a **Glazier**, your task is to repair all windscreens and other windows, making sure that they fit safely into the frames,

which often involves restoring them as well. You'll be cutting glass to fit as well as using pre-prepared units.

6. Being a **Trimmer** is rather like being a furniture restorer. Your task here is to repair all the furnishings and fittings inside motor vehicles and restore them to their former glory.

Not all repairs can be carried out in the garage, at least not in the first instance. When cars break down at the side of the road, their drivers often need the help of a breakdown recovery service, either from a garage in the area or from one of the national organisations, such as the AA, RAC or Green Flag.

1. The job of the **Roadside Recovery Technician** is to get to the scene of the accident or breakdown as quickly as possible, make sure everything is safe and then arrange for damaged or broken down vehicles to be removed, often by towing to the nearest garage.

2. Although many of the priorities of the **Roadside Assistance Technician** are the same, the essence of this role is to provide an instant repair service if at all possible. So the focus is on trying to enable the owner to drive the vehicle from the scene rather than provide a towing service.

As is the case with most mechanical items, maintenance is a high priority for motor vehicles because of the amount of wear and tear they sustain. This is why there is now a whole range of fitting services available.

1. Specialist garages provide rapid replacement services to the general public for items such as clutches, brakes etc. If

you want to work in one of these, or there is room for such a specialist at a general repairs garage, you could become a **Fast-Fit Technician**, concentrating on providing a swift response to customers, often while they're waiting.

2. The sophistication of in-car technology is advancing all the time, especially in the areas of sound, security and tracking traffic, so there is now a specific job of **Mobile Electronics and Security Technician**, where you advise on, and install, all the relevant and varied systems chosen by customers.

3. Another example of workshops offering customers a limited yet focused service is the tyre shop, where you can find a job as a **Specialist Tyre Fitter**, checking and replacing tyres and balancing wheels.

4. Finally, all vehicles need spare parts and a large sub-industry has grown up supplying these. Getting them to the right place at the right time is the job of the **Vehicle Parts Operative**. You'll find that this role demands considerable computer skills to deal with all the stock control systems and requires you to be organised, efficient and sufficiently knowledgeable to be able to advise people on the parts they'll need.

RUNNING A MOTOR VEHICLE BUSINESS

Like all other businesses, companies in the motor industry need expert management and sound administration if they are to prosper. Many of these jobs are exactly the same as those in other industries with the result that it is easier for people to come into the industry if they have these skills – and to transfer out if they so wish. Apparently, there are 45,089 garage managers/proprietors in Britain.

1. If you want to get into the motor industry and you have secretarial skills but nothing else apart from enthusiasm, then you could become a **Secretary**. The duties are similar to those in any line of business, which enables you to transfer in and out of the industry with ease.

2. Another starter job is that of **Service Receptionist**, where your duties will put you in constant contact with customers. As a result, you'll have to be cool under pressure, well organised and a very good communicator.

3. The other, more general, junior administrative role is that of **Department Assistant**. Your principal aim will be to support the manager, but with a secondary aim of grooming yourself for management. The industry has departmental functions, such as personnel and finance, which are also common to most other industries.

> ## DID YOU KNOW?
>
> A dealership is a garage that has a licence either to sell a certain make of car, or any type of car, to the general public once the car has been bought from the manufacturer. Many dealerships are therefore closely linked to manufacturers.

4. Once you have proved yourself in a supporting role, then the way may become clear for you to be a **Department Manager**. Your priorities will be similar to those in management in other industries, although you will be expected to acquire a large fund of vehicle-related knowledge rapidly.

5. The ultimate goal for all managers, whether in the administration support functions or in sales or marketing, is

to become **Managing Director** or **Dealer Principal** – the person in charge of a dealership. If you're lucky enough to be promoted to the top of the tree, you'll find that the job is particularly concerned with people management and motivation, creating the right conditions for the skills of all your team to flourish.

CHANGES TO THE MOT

Annual MOT tests for cars could well be scrapped after a Treasury review of EU red tape. The study found that Britain's 22 million motorists would save £465 million a year if they had the MOT test less frequently, and that there would be no obvious decrease in road safety. The MOT test system, established in 1968, is the second toughest in the EU, with only Latvia having tighter controls. Drivers must get an MOT test when a car is three years old, but if the starting point was four years rather than three, drivers would save £80 million a year in fees and if subsequent MOTs happened every other year rather than annually, even more money would be saved. Treasury officials said that they would consult police and road safety groups before going ahead with the reform and that it would take about a year to come into effect.

Tools of the trade

Now that you've seen in broad outline why working in the motor industry might be an excellent career opportunity, it's probably time to assess the qualities you'll need in order to make that career a successful one.

These general qualities apply to all or most jobs in the trade and it is a good idea to check whether you have them before embarking on a job in the motor industry. You could look at them as your personal tools to advancement.

- It almost goes without saying that being **good with your hands** is a definite advantage for every job in the manufacturing and maintenance areas of the industry. Of course these are skills that you can learn but it is much easier if you possess the right sort of manual dexterity in the first place.
  Even if you want to take up a role in sales and marketing, administration or finance work, or if you see yourself in management, it will do you no harm whatsoever if you are able to undertake basic engine repairs. The more you know about what's going on under the bonnet, and how it works, the better. All knowledge can be put to good use.

- It doesn't matter whether you are working in a dealership, a workshop or an independent garage, as long as you are **practical**. You may dream of designing the world's lightest or quietest car but there will be no market for it if it doesn't work. You may wish to sell every customer a top-of-the-range sports car, but if they are a family of five with two dogs, what they really need is a people carrier. Having common sense and a practical outlook will really help you to advance.

- Whatever job you decide to go for, you'll always find that being **mentally agile** and quick to pick things up is a definite bonus. There are so many possibilities you have to deal with, whether you're tinkering in a workshop or spending most of your time behind a desk, that it'll help you greatly if you can run through all the likely causes and outcomes as quickly as possible. This is because the situation will be changing constantly. Certainly there are some routines that will become fixed points of the day, but at all other times you'll need to be flexible and ready to adapt to each set of circumstances.

- All aspects of education are clearly helpful to you in your career but, if there's any one subject that all people in the motor industry are likely to use a lot, you'll find it's **mathematics**. Whether you're totting up sales figures or calculating wages, good attention to your maths studies at school and college is bound to add up in your favour. It'll be of great practical value.

- As an adjunct to your experience of maths, if you aspire to a job in, say, repairs or manufacturing, you should have a sound knowledge of the **basic principles of physics**. Similarly, if you want to get involved in design and engineering, you'll have to take your understanding of theory and practice to a much higher level.

- No one works in isolation in the motor industry. You'll have to demonstrate that you can get on with people at all levels because, whatever your job, you're liable to be working in a series of teams. Even expert mechanics, designers and engineers need to be **able to communicate** constantly. Again, it is possible to develop such skills once you're in work, although it may be fair to say that good personal relationships and interaction stem from having the right attitude.
- Because it's a trade in which communication is clearly so important, you'll discover that having a good sense of humour is a great advantage. Sometimes, when things have gone wrong (as they invariably do in any walk of life), it's an absolute necessity.

  Busy places like assembly and production lines, repair workshops and sales offices are terrific breeding grounds for jokes and witty repartee, and often function all the better for it. This is not to say that every job is casual and a laugh a minute. People in the industry are professional and know that doing their tasks to the best of their ability comes first.
- Whatever career you wish to pursue, finding out what the customer really wants and delivering that to him or her is at the core of your work. As a result, anyone who stops to make time for customers or work colleagues is quickly going to demonstrate how useful they are. As with clear communication and skills in personal relationships, **good customer care** is the result of a natural attitude of mind, albeit one that you can also develop in the job.
- Again, this may seem obvious, but a lot of the work involved is painstaking and finicky, demanding a great deal of **patience**. You may be engaged in a particularly

tricky aspect of designing or making a vehicle, or trying very hard to replace an especially small and inaccessible part. On the other hand, you could be dealing with a customer who seems pathologically unable to make a decision or wrestling with a more than usually difficult problem of man management.

Although you have to be decisive yourself, it is better not to rush into action until you're sure you've got things absolutely right. It's not good enough to be almost right when, to take an extreme example, people's lives might be at stake.

- If you're hoping to work in any of the non-office jobs connected with the motor industry, then being **physically fit** and having good upper body strength is a distinct advantage. Many of the tasks involved in repair and maintenance (and some in manufacturing) are physically demanding. Even sales professionals, who may have to spend a lot of time on their feet, need stamina and fitness, as do other members of the management and administration teams.

- Many of the jobs in the industry can be performed more swiftly and efficiently if you can retain a **clear memory** of what has happened before in similar situations. Generally the work is not repetitive, but certain problems are bound to arise more than once and you can deal with them better if you can recall what has worked successfully before.

Of course you can develop these skills further while you're doing the job, but it is useful to have trained your brain to remember various facts and details to pass examinations at school and college.

- In addition to physical stamina, it's important that you have the mental stamina to be able to cope with

working under pressure. Although the consequences of getting things wrong are less catastrophic than, for example, in heart surgery, there is still regular and consistent pressure that can be a test of mental strength. The pressure of exams may be the only direct experience you have if you're new to working life. Many of you will be able to manage easily and some may even prefer working under the added stimulus of pressure.

- **Learning to drive** has a whole host of benefits for working in many sides of the business. It goes without saying that you will have to be a very competent driver if you wish to be a Driving Instructor, a Roadside Recovery Technician or even a Salesperson who has to take people out to test drive cars. The more you know about your product the better it is for you, so being able to drive is a powerful tool for you to possess.

Now that we have covered some of the positive attributes that will help you to succeed in the industry, there are a few conditions that might have a negative influence on whether or not you can do so.

- If you suffer from a **fear of confined spaces**, then it is probably best not to seek work in the repair or maintenance side of the business. Although many workshops are quite large, the potential for working in cramped areas is always there. If you are determined on a career in those sides of the business, perhaps you should try to cure or alleviate your condition first.
- A great deal of the work involved in building or repairing vehicles brings you close to malfunctioning engines and exhausts, which means you might be subjected to

noxious fumes. Alternatively, you may have to use equipment that can affect the atmosphere, such as blowtorches, paints and other sprays. If you have **asthmaor any other breathing difficulty**, you are likely to be badly affected by these changes to the air quality. Again, seek a cure or some handy assistance (e.g. an inhaler for asthma or a special mask) if you're set on trying this type of work.

- Although wearing glasses or contact lenses means you can make up for any **eyesight deficiencies**, the nature of much of the manufacturing and repair work on vehicles tends to put excessive strain on the eyes. If your eyes are especially sensitive, you may find that the type of precise work you have to do in the industry can cause you further problems. Consult an optician for advice if you feel your eyes may be at risk.
- Similarly, most of the work, whether in the workshop, office or production and assembly lines, does require that you concentrate fully at all times. If you have any problems with **maintaining awareness and concentration** for whatever reason, the consequences could be dangerous. For instance, you might be working with potentially lethal equipment and a sudden lapse of concentration could be fatal to you or others. Your doctor may be able to prescribe some medication to offset such problems.

● If you have difficulties **keeping track of the time**, either when you're working to a deadline or when you're due at your particular place of work, it goes without saying that this will not help you to advance in the industry (or even keep you in it for very long).

This is true for work in all types of business, but particularly in the motor industry where so many actions and reactions (in manufacturing jobs, for instance) depend on precise timing. The only real solution is to get a watch and train yourself to arrive ten minutes early.

QUIZ

WHAT ARE YOU LIKE?

Now that we've looked at the qualities you will need in this trade, why not try this quick, fun quiz to see if you are suited to working in the motor industry. Just mark whether you think each statement is true or false.

I like to see the results of my work in action
TRUE/FALSE

I believe I have a feel for vehicles and engines
TRUE/FALSE

I think first-rate customer service is one of my main concerns
TRUE/FALSE

I like dealing with different problems each day
TRUE/FALSE

I think teamwork is important in the work I do
TRUE/FALSE

Working with my hands gives me great satisfaction
TRUE/FALSE

Transport is more than just a means of getting around
TRUE/FALSE

If you've marked all or most of these statements as being TRUE, you've probably got the right temperament to work in the motor industry.

If you've marked all or most of them as being FALSE, then you may not be cut out to work on vehicles but you might want to consider an administrative or supporting role.

If there is a fairly even split, then you should think hard about which route you really want to take – read on to see what working in the industry is really like before deciding.

Real lives

In this section, some people who have worked in the motor trade for different lengths of time tell you just what you can expect at each stage of your career.

These case studies range from a person still at school, to those who have started recently at college or as vehicle technicians, and right up to experienced mechanics running their own business.

DONALD PEARCE – VEHICLE TECHNICIAN

Donald was one of the first to qualify as an Apprentice Technician.

'It was a good training and I'm glad I did it. Sometimes I felt things were going a little slowly, but perhaps that's just me. Overall, it was very useful.'

The time Donald spent working in a dealership ended sooner than for most – but not everyone gets the opportunity to take over a going concern as he did.

'Even though I'm now working for myself, it was good to have gained some experience of working for others. The fact

Even though I'm now working for myself, it was good to have gained some experience of working for others

that I was in employment really helped me to form my thoughts about what I wanted to do, and as a result I decided to take the chance to set up in business for myself.'

Donald now runs his own repair workshop in west London.

'I might go back and do the supervisory and management levels someday, but the difficulty is finding the time. Once you've set up on your own, any time you spend away from the garage is time when you could be earning, so it becomes hard.'

LEE WETHERSPOON – STUDYING CITY & GUILDS

Lee Wetherspoon left school recently and is now studying for her Level 1, Motor Vehicle City & Guilds certificate at Motherwell College in Scotland.

What made you choose the motor industry?
I've always been interested in working with cars. My dad has a garage, and I've been helping him since quite an early age, so it seemed the natural thing to do.

What is the college training like?
It's very good, just what I expected. I'm studying full-time, which means I go to the college four days a week. I should have completed the course in two years.

When do you hope to start the practical aspects of training?
At the moment I'm planning to begin when I've finished my studies, but I probably won't be working in my father's garage. I think it's best to complete my training elsewhere.

What are the best things (and the worst) about your studies?
I can honestly say that I like it all so there's no low point, but nothing particularly stands out for me so far.

How do you find working in a male-dominated industry?
No problem – there's another woman in the year above me, so I'm not totally alone, but it's really not an issue.

Have you any advice for school-leavers wishing to enter the trade?
It's great so far. I'd recommend it to anyone.

JAMIE'S STORY* – HOW CONNEXIONS CAN HELP

Jamie Wilson was a 14-year-old in a fix. He was doing well at school but did not know what he wanted to do as a career and was particularly nervous because he realised that the choices he made could affect the rest of his life.

Jamie's mum was concerned that he had not made any decisions about his future, so she had been in contact with the school about his GCSE subjects. The school arranged for Jamie to have a chat with the Connexions Personal Adviser, Wendy.

'I was really worried as I needed to think about which GCSE subjects I was going to study, but I didn't know where to start. Nothing seemed to be going right and I was confused about what I wanted – until I spoke to the Connexions Personal Adviser. I'm a lot happier now and have even started enjoying school – just a little bit!'

* Grateful acknowledgement is made to Connexions for permission to use this case study from their website www.connexions.co.uk

The Connexions service has been set up specifically to offer advice and support to those aged 13 and beyond. Jamie and Wendy talked about his interests and it turned out that, in his spare time, he was restoring a classic car with his dad.

They discussed a possible career as a car mechanic and Jamie was really interested, so Wendy arranged for him to spend a week at a local garage during the Easter holidays to gain some work experience.

DID YOU KNOW?

Three times more women qualified to be vehicle technicians in 2003 than in 2002, according to City & Guilds, one of the UK's leading awarding bodies.

By the end of the week Jamie realised that this was what he wanted to do. Back at school, he spoke to Wendy again and decided to plan towards working with cars as a career. He chose GCSE subjects that reflected this and is now a lot happier and more relaxed about the matter with a plan in place.

'Wendy was really helpful with the work experience placement. I thoroughly enjoyed it – in fact, I think they were quite impressed with my knowledge of cars. After my week there, the manager offered me Saturday work, helping out, cleaning cars and doing small jobs, so I'm getting a bit of money and also picking up some experience to add to my CV.'

WESLEY DEADMAN – REPAIR GARAGE OWNER

Wesley Deadman runs RB Motor Services in Croydon, south London, a garage that specialises in providing maintenance and repair services for limousines and hearses, although it also offers these services to owners of more conventional vehicles.

His Apprenticeship in the industry was less formal than would be the case today, but his views on the way things are going are clear and forceful.

I was thrown in at the deep end, which is normal if you're working in a small garage.

Why did you choose the motor industry?
I expect I was like a lot of young men when I was 17 in that I was hugely interested in cars and what made them tick. Where I was different was that my father ran a garage, so you'd think it might have been easy for me. Not a bit of it – he said he didn't want me to go into the business at the time. So I worked for about 18 months as a kitchen fitter, but I really wasn't happy and knew I still wanted to be a mechanic.

How did you get your first job – and what was it?
Well, eventually I persuaded my dad that it was right for me to join, so that's what happened. Basically he put me to work on anything and everything. I was thrown in at the deep end, which is normal if you're working in a small garage. I was put to work on vehicles straightaway although I had someone supervising me, but it was a case of training on the job.

You'll find that if you start an Apprenticeship in a big garage or one of the large dealerships, then you'll have a structured programme that teaches you some theory before you begin practical work. Also, they tend to specialise in various makes and systems, so the work you do is restricted, but you do become expert in those areas quite quickly.

The type of Apprenticeship I had was much broader, less structured, but it was a great way to find out a fair amount about nearly all types of vehicle.

Can you summarise a typical working day?
The thing is there's probably no such thing as a typical day – the problems and the vehicles change so much from one day to the next. I have to spend a lot of time dealing with customers and there are just so many varied things they need doing to their cars that each day is different.

The motor trade has altered a great deal in the last 20 years, because now there are so many more fitters and replacers taking out old items and fitting new ones. This is because it's not thought to be cost-effective or worthwhile for technicians to repair various faulty parts. So whereas people used to do both jobs, they don't always do so now.

What are the best things about your job?
I suppose the best feelings are those glows of satisfaction that come when I've solved a particularly tricky or niggling problem. I prefer getting an old unit to function effectively rather than throwing it away and replacing it.

I suppose the best feelings are those glows of satisfaction that come when I've solved a particularly tricky or niggling problem

What are the worst things about your job?
Perhaps the worst part is having to explain to customers that more work is needed on their vehicles. I'd say that the

majority of jobs are ones that customers didn't realise were necessary. They bring in their vehicle for one problem, but that's had a knock-on effect and other problems have cropped up. The trouble is that, whereas people will happily spend money on comfort and speed – say £1,000 on a flash stereo system – they'll resent having to spend a quarter of that on essential maintenance and safety.

Have you any advice for school-leavers wishing to enter the trade?
Yes, the way things are going, I think they should get in with one of the established main dealers. They should try and start one of the Apprenticeships and specialise in particular types of vehicles or systems because that's the way of the future. The supply of spare parts is going to become more and more restrictive, and that's going to work in favour of the larger garages.

Can you identify any qualities that make people more likely to succeed?
The first quality anyone needs is reliability, because so much depends on your work. By the same token, you need to be exceptionally safety conscious and you must always be thorough in all your work. You have to have good listening skills to hear what customers are telling you, and be able to interpret that into the work you do. You should always be honest and trustworthy in all your dealings. Finally, you must be presentable, even if you don't mind getting your hands dirty.

What do you think the future holds for you and the industry?
I think that some of the backstreet garages might have problems keeping up with the pace of technological change

in the industry – so much of it is tied up with computerisation and diagnostics already and that trend is only going to increase. However, the prospects for hard-working, well-trained individuals are good, because there is actually a shortage of decent people and there will always be room for more. So I'd advise anyone to get a proper training and go for it.

STEVE PEARCE – MOTORCYCLE TECHNICIAN/MOTOCROSS RIDER

Eighteen-year-old Steve Pearce is currently doing an Advanced Apprenticeship in Motorcycle Mechanics, training to be a Motorcycle Technician.

He has been interested in motorbikes since he was about 11. When he was 12 he got his first bike, which he rode in his grandfather's fields. At 14 he managed to persuade his dad to come to a motocross meeting to watch, which his father really enjoyed and within a couple of months they bought a newer bike as the original one wasn't suitable for competitive racing. Steve then joined a club and started racing. He entered his first race in the Junior Class in September 2002 at the age of 14 and worked through the classes over the next couple of years and is now in the top five of the North Avon/South Gloucestershire Championships. Steve is doing his Advanced Apprenticeship with a local firm.

'In April 2003 I had my Year 10 work experience with a motorcycle dealer as my hobby involved motorbikes. At the end of the week the owner of the showroom and workshop offered me an Apprenticeship. I still had a year left at school but was very excited about this offer as it gave me a focus to obtain the qualifications I needed to be able to start the

Apprenticeship. To get into the college I needed to attain Grade C in English, maths and science, which I achieved.'

If Steve had failed to get the relevant GCSE grades he could have gone on to achieve equivalent exams at college, however as he already had them it meant he's been able to concentrate on getting through the rest of the course.

'So far I have my Level 2 qualification and am half way through my third and final year which, if I pass this year's exams and assessments, will give me an NVQ in Vehicle and Maintenance Repair at Level 3. The main benefit of doing the course will be the experience. The more experience I can get the better because I'll become more proficient. It's not just learning how to diagnose faults and fix the bikes, I am also learning how to run the business. The certification will support any further job applications and give me more credibility if I ever decide to start up a business on my own.

I know that being on an Apprenticeship that is sending me to college is a large benefit

'My main job role is servicing and repairs. Services are routine annual checks and generally just require replacing wear and tear parts. The more interesting part of the job is diagnosing a fault from scratch and rectifying it. It can be annoying when a fault is hard to diagnose but on the other hand if they were all straightforward it wouldn't give me the same satisfaction when it goes well. That's what I enjoy most about the job – the job satisfaction. I enjoy solving problems and being able to fix them. When the bike goes back to the owner fixed I feel I've achieved something. I also enjoy earning while I learn, although the pay isn't very good it still gives me a bit of independence. Also I know that being on an Apprenticeship that is sending me to college is a large benefit.

'At the moment I think I'd like to one day own my own shop with a workshop and showroom. I've not given it too much thought yet, I need to concentrate on my Apprenticeship and get a few more years experience under my belt before I'll know if this is definitely what I want to do. Then I'll be able to think about making more long-term decisions like running my own business.'

KEVIN MCENTEE – MOTORCYCLE TECHNICIAN

Twenty-two-year-old Kevin has had a passion for motorcycles from about the age of 13.

He used to sneak off on his pushbike to go to local motocross events and while all the other kids had Spice Girls posters on their walls, he had a poster of Ricky Carmichael, the Suzuki motocrosser. He left school with two Fs at GCSE but knew he wanted to do something practical and he has just completed a three year Suzuki Advanced Modern Apprenticeship programme, which gives him the required NVQs to work in any motorcycle dealership. Kevin has also twice been the runner up in the Suzuki Apprentice of the Year competition.

'I did my work experience at Rob Willsher Motorcycles, my local motorcycle shop, in Hampshire. I enjoyed my time there and they offered me a Saturday job, helping out. That led to me starting full-time employment at the same shop when I left school. An opportunity arose for me to join the Suzuki

Modern Apprentice scheme, which is a course specifically for the motorcycle trade. Whilst doing the Apprenticeship I was able to carry out tasks that I would not normally experience in day-to-day work and I was able to understand and to have practical help understanding how things work. I was then able to come back to the workplace and put theory into practice.'

Kevin started his Apprenticeship learning how to build the knock down bikes from the crates in which they are delivered from Japan, including fitting the tyres and the handlebars. Now he is servicing, maintaining and repairing all Suzuki Motorcycles. The work is varied and ranges from basic service work to fault finding and sorting out running problems. Most bikes now have engine management systems that require being connected to a laptop to set up, so the work is varied.

'I like being able to work with bikes and being able to ride all sorts of different bikes. In the past few years I've probably ridden every bike Suzuki have made. But I don't enjoy road testing in the rain and cold. It's great fun in the summer but not so much fun in the winter!'

Ultimately, Kevin would like to work up to Service Manager level. When he was younger he wanted to be a race team mechanic but has since discovered how much hard work that is with an awful lot of pressure. He says in order to be good at what he does you need to be able to communicate with work colleagues and customers alike; being able to explain yourself. You also need the ability to be able to interpret exactly what the customer wants. Most importantly you need to be committed to your profession.

'This is hard, dirty work, with poor pay until you qualify. And it's not all about working on nice clean shiny new bikes; the reality is that 75 per cent of the bikes that come in are three or more years old, are dirty and not very well looked after with seized and rusted fixings. Also, jobs are not easy to find in this trade; most of the people on my course all started the same way as I did, either by work experience or by Saturday jobs. But it is very enjoyable and rewarding.'

The Suzuki Advanced Modern Apprenticeship programme is run by EMTEC, who are part of the Carter & Carter Group. They are based in Nottingham and they run courses for Suzuki and most of the major manufacturers in the motor and motorcycle trades. They can be contacted on 0115 846 1200 or have a look at their website www.emtec-training. co.uk/index2.htm.

Making your mind up

It's almost coming to crunch time – do you feel that you've gathered enough information about the industry to commit yourself to training for the qualifications that will help you be successful? Just before we examine the ways in which you can get into the industry and how to gain those all-important qualifications, it might be a good time to pause and consider your options before moving on.

You now know a bit more about the industry in general and about individual jobs within the industry in particular. You've learned a little about the qualities, both positive and negative, that will assist or hinder you. Perhaps a few questions remain at the back of your mind – about pay, conditions, perceptions and commitment. Here are the answers to the most commonly asked questions about the motor industry.

HOW LONG DO I HAVE TO TRAIN FOR?

There is no set length of training because, at one end of the scale, engineering degrees may take up to five years to complete, whereas a secretarial course may take just a few weeks or months. However, if you're considering trying to pass an NVQ Level 1 or 2, it will take two to three years, and progressing to Level 3 should take a further year to 18 months. Training for such qualifications is discussed in detail in Chapter 6.

WHAT'S THE PAY LIKE?

Good. If you work in sales, you'll find that a proportion of your wages depends on commission, so the more cars or parts you sell, the more you earn. For everyone else, pay compares well with jobs in similar industries. While you're training for a job in the repair and maintenance sector, you'll be paid at rates agreed by the Joint Industry Board (JIB). Once you've qualified, you will be able to enter the JIB grading structure, which links pay and conditions to the level of qualifications and experience.

As a general guideline, you can expect to be earning an annual salary of up to £20,000, increasing up to £30,000 for some positions after a company has employed you for a couple of years. While you're qualifying you would obviously be earning less than that. For example, a Motor Vehicle Technician will start on around £10,500 as a new trainee, while an Auto Electrician earns approximately £12,000 as an Apprentice and a Vehicle Breakdown Engineer starts on a salary of around £15,000.

You can expect to be earning an annual salary of up to £20,000, increasing up to £30,000 for some positions after a company has employed you for a couple of years

WILL I HAVE A NORMAL WORKING WEEK?

Yes, you usually do, varying from eight to ten hours each day at the normal times, depending on the terms of your contract, although there is obviously some shift work involved in manufacturing and breakdown repairs. There may also be some work on Saturday mornings for repair and maintenance employees, and some sales and marketing people will have to work all through the weekend (probably on a rota system) because that is the only time when many potential customers can view and test drive vehicles.

Those working with breakdown services, such as the AA, may find themselves working extremely strange hours as a 24-hour service is offered – if someone breaks down on the M25 at three o'clock in the morning, they still have to be assisted.

WHAT ABOUT HOLIDAYS?

Holidays are pretty standard, offering an average of four working weeks each year, as well as all the public holidays (Christmas, New Year, Easter and bank holidays). Many companies will also offer extra days depending on the length of service, so your entitlement may rise to five weeks, or above, the longer you stay with the same employer.

Many of the skills that you learn in the industry are readily transferable, such as those in management, administration or sales and marketing

CAN I CHANGE CAREERS EASILY?

Yes, you can. As you will have discovered, many of the skills that you learn in the industry are readily transferable, such as those in management, administration or sales and marketing. However, even specialist skills that are useful in manufacturing – for instance, engineering and craftsmanship – or in repair and maintenance can help you to change career. For example, you might be able to take on work as an electrician if you've worked on auto electrics, as a glazier if you've worked on windscreen and window repairs, or as an upholsterer if you've had a job as a car interior trimmer.

CAN I WORK ABROAD?

You are permitted to work in any country that is a member of the European Union (although obviously being able to speak the relevant foreign language will help). If you want to try this out, there is a Young Workers' Exchange Programme (for ages 18–28) which will give you work experience or training in the country of your choice for as little as three weeks or up to 16 months. There are no such guarantees for other parts of the world, but if you have some solid qualifications behind you, that should stand you in good stead.

WHAT ARE THE PROMOTION PROSPECTS?

Promotion prospects are very good indeed within all the areas of the industry. Obviously a great deal, if not all, depends on you. If you work and study hard, complete your training swiftly, develop your expertise and show willingness to do more than is necessary, you'll get on just fine.

You'll find a discussion of some typical promotional career paths in Chapter 7.

WHAT DOES THE PUBLIC THINK OF THE INDUSTRY?

The popular perception of the motor industry is pretty good. The public's view of the manufacturing side has changed a lot (as has the industry) since the strike-riddled days of the 1970s, although some lingering feelings and conditioned responses may remain. As for working in the maintenance and repair sides of the industry, the individual views of members of the public may be coloured by any unfortunate experiences they have had.

Naturally, TV programmes and newspaper articles tend to dwell on cowboy garages and things that have gone wrong. So the position is probably a mixed one, although it is generally fair to say that most people realise customer service standards are improving.

By the same token, the popular view of those involved in sales and marketing can tend to fluctuate wildly. On the one hand, there are still the jokes about second-hand car salesmen, finding their strangest expression in the character and ramblings of Swiss Tony in *The Fast Show*. On the other hand, the popularity of Jeremy Clarkson, a salesman in disguise, and motoring programmes such as *Top Gear* show that a large proportion of the public enjoys the hype and techno-babble of certain sales techniques.

Finally, there is a very good public feeling towards members of the breakdown service organisations, brought about for the obvious reason that they're always helping people when they're in some distress.

WHAT WILL I GET OUT OF IT APART FROM A CAREER?

Three main things: a strong feeling of satisfaction and self-worth, a chance to meet a broad cross-section of people, and – not to be dismissed – the knowledge that your own motoring needs should be largely taken care of.

CASTROL BUSINESS SERVICES CAR REPAIR TREND TRACKER REPORT 2006

Independent garages account for 47 per cent of all work carried out on cars in the UK, while franchised main dealers account for 25 per cent and fast-fit outlets for 9 per cent. But independent garages are revealed to be losing market share to fast-fit outlets, with franchised dealers holding steady.

Trend Tracker analyst Robert Macnab comments: 'The core advantage of independent garages over franchised main dealers is their lower overheads and lower pricing structures, but as cars become more technically complex, independent garages will need to reassure owners of younger cars that they are technically competent to work on more sophisticated vehicles.'

Fourteen per cent of 18,000 motorists surveyed for the Car Repair Trend Tracker over the January 2005–June 2006 period had a service, MOT or repair carried out to their vehicle within the previous month. That equates to a total of 5.0 million jobs, of which 2.58 million were repairs, 1.25 million were services, and 1.17 million were MOT tests. As the average age of cars reduces and they have longer service intervals and generally become more durable, volume demand for servicing, MOTs and repairs is steadily falling, despite an increase in the number of cars in the UK.

Source: The 2006 Castrol Business Services Car Repair Trend Tracker report, published by Trend Tracker Ltd

If you're involved in the repair, maintenance or breakdown recovery side, you'll get a feeling of satisfaction from knowing that you've helped people in one of the most important aspects of their daily lives. If you're involved in manufacturing, sales or administration, you'll know you've helped to deliver state-of-the-art vehicles to your customers.

Furthermore, whatever your role in the industry, you'll invariably be meeting many different people. As in the rest of life, you probably won't want to be friends with them all, but communicating with each and every one of them will be interesting on many different levels.

6

Training day

Although it is possible to enter the motor industry with no set entry qualifications, you will advance much more quickly if you show a certain level of academic achievement. For example, for most training courses you will need at least four GCSEs and good subjects to take are maths, physics and a practical subject, such as woodwork or metalwork. 'What we suffer from is slightly less able students being pointed in the direction of the motor industry almost as a default or as a last resort,' explains Dominic Luddy of Automotive Skills. 'Unfortunately, we are getting a lot of people who are not capable of handling the high levels of technology involved and they are either taken on and are then disappointed because they can't cope with the demands placed on them or they are rejected outright.'

However, if you feel you have the necessary skills to make a success of a career in the motor industry then the way in which you train will very much depend on what level you wish to attain. For example, for the more highly qualified roles of engineer, designer or marketing specialist, most people train for a degree or BTEC/SQA higher national qualification such as Motor Vehicle Management and Technology. If you are already a graduate, you can join a graduate training scheme and progress via in-house training. 'We need more graduate level engineering students coming into the industry,' says Dominic, 'they can do very well in the motor trade doing diagnostics.'

APRENTICESHIPS

For craftspeople and technicians the main qualifications for the motor industry are the Apprenticeship in England and Wales, or Modern Apprenticeship (also sometimes known as Skillseekers) in Scotland, and the Advanced Apprenticeship in England. (The latter is known as the Modern Apprenticeship in Wales and Scotland.) In both cases, you have to do some on-the-job training with a company and some theoretical training at college. This can be done on a day-release or block-release basis.

One of the crucial benefits is that you earn as you learn. Naturally your salary will not be as high as when you qualify, but it should give you a terrific incentive to complete your studies successfully and as quickly as possible. It's best to do the practical and theoretical stages at the same time because it helps you to relate all the pieces of learning to each other.

These programmes will be run either by an employer, such as Daewoo or Vauxhall, or in association with an organisation such as Automotive Skills (formerly the Motor Industry Training Council), the Sector Skills Council for the motor industry, which works with employers to provide training, or the Institute of the Motor Industry (IMI).

Apprenticeships and Advanced Apprenticeships lead to a National Vocational Qualification (NVQ) or Scottish Vocational Qualification (SVQ) in all the necessary subjects. It usually takes between two and three years to gain an Apprenticeship, leading to NVQ/SVQ Levels 1 and 2, while an Advanced Apprenticeship takes a further 18 months and leads to NVQ/SVQ Level 3.

Most of these Apprenticeships are designed for school-leavers and young people aged between 16 and 24 and are fully funded up to the age of 19. It is possible for more mature candidates to be accepted and you can get some subsidy to help with your training between the ages of 19 and 24 but after 24 you get no financial help at all (this is not true in Scotland where Adult Apprenticeships are available). Sometimes you can get local initiatives or some of the larger employees will fund adult training, but this is rare.

The skill levels in NVQ/SVQ terms broadly correspond to:

- Level 1 – Basic skills, with an introduction to your chosen topic
- Level 2 – Completion of Foundation skills
- Level 3 – Advanced skills, to give you specialist knowledge
- Level 4 – Supervisory skills, or very advanced technical skills
- Level 5 – Managerial skills for those who want to progress further.

For very talented 14- to 16-year-olds there is also the Young Apprenticeship programme. Here, the majority of the student's time will be spent in school studying the core curriculum, then for two days a week he/she goes to college or a motor vehicle training centre to work towards a Level 2 NVQ delivered through a Young Apprenticeship Partnership.

You can find lists of possible companies and colleges offering on-the-job training at www.automotiveskills.org.uk. Alternatively, scour your local phone book for possibilities. It's probably a good idea to keep a record of the progress of all your enquiries.

If you cannot find a position on a training course that suits you, it might be possible to join a company, establish yourself in the job, and then start your formal training later.

TRAINING PROVIDERS

CITY & GUILDS
As you'd expect from the main provider of training resources in the UK, City & Guilds offers you a vast array of potential qualifications in the motor vehicle servicing and repair fields. In fact, it supplies 65 per cent of the qualifications. It has a scheme operating on five different levels that correspond fairly closely to NVQs/SVQs. (More details are given in the Resources section.)

THE INSTITUTE OF THE MOTOR INDUSTRY
If you're having problems finding a course you want to take, you can try applying directly to the IMI. Their qualifications – mainly Automotive Technician Accreditation – are Government funded for those under 25 years old and are pitched at similar levels to NVQs and SVQs. The IMI has 35 per cent of the motor industry market with over 45,000 students.

Their pre-apprenticeship programmes are especially useful if you're struggling to find work experience. Go to their website at www.motor.org.uk to find out more.

HNC/HND COURSES
Edexcel still administers the Higher National Certificate (HNC) and Higher National Diploma (HND) awards. You are eligible to study for these if you've passed your A-levels (or Highers in Scotland).

Most of the HNC and HND courses relating to the motor industry are in the business, technical and engineering areas. Again, they combine practical work with theory. There are more details in the Resources section, or look at the website for the Department of Trade and Industry (www.dti.gov.uk), which has a list of the current education institutes and offers a searchable database of courses.

HOW TO GET ACCEPTED ON A TRAINING PROGRAMME

There are five main ways of being taken on for training:

- You are nominated by a national training provider
- You are nominated by a local training provider
- You are nominated by a careers service/Connexions
- You are nominated by your local employment agency
- You are nominated by your employer.

All routes require you to take some action on your own behalf.

NATIONAL TRAINING PROVIDERS

Each country in the UK has a designated national training provider for the profession. These set out the overall plans and guidelines. Automotive Skills is responsible for skills development throughout the UK and, in conjunction with various national bodies, forms these plans.

LOCAL TRAINING PROVIDERS

Each country in the UK is subdivided into smaller areas, where the advisers will know in greater detail what is happening in your area. Look for the Learning and Skills Councils for England, Scottish Enterprise and their local enterprise councils for Scotland and, in Wales, Education and Learning Wales.

CAREERS SERVICES
Both your local and your school careers services can refer you for training in the profession if you can demonstrate that you have the potential to succeed.

CONNEXIONS
Connexions is the government's support service for all young people aged between 13 and 19 in England. It can give you advice and help on starting your career and offer you personal development opportunities. To find out more, go to www.connexions.gov.uk. (See also the Resources section.)

LOCAL EMPLOYMENT AGENCY
Your JobCentre or local employment agency can refer you for training in the profession. Again, you must show you have the potential to succeed.

EMPLOYERS
You can take the initiative and, if you are already in work, convince your employer to apply for you to go on training courses. Alternatively, you can approach prospective employers and undertake to carry out the training as a condition of employment.

WHAT ARE THE BENEFITS OF GETTING TRAINING?
Because of the way the industry is rapidly embracing new technology it is becoming harder and harder to succeed in the motor industry without proper qualifications, and even those who've managed to do so in the past are now

recommending that it is preferable to follow the training route.

The reasons are not hard to fathom. Employers need to be able to rely on the people they take on and having qualifications (or studying for them) are significant evidence that you can do a good job for them. From your own point of view, having proof that you've acquired these skills (or are in the process of acquiring them) gives you a sound basis for your career, making it far easier for you to change jobs if necessary.

GRADUATE BENEFITS AND OPPORTUNITIES

Generally, the learning you pick up from studying for a degree will be immensely helpful in the future. Whether you've been taking an all-purpose engineering course or one of the specialist automotive degrees available, you'll be gathering useful knowledge every day.

There are some specialist postgraduate courses you can attend to learn more about the industry with plenty of practical content

When you've got your degree, several choices are open to you. There are some specialist postgraduate courses you can attend to learn more about the industry with plenty of practical content. Or you could follow the designated 'autoroute' path, a scheme for graduates looking for professional training, which in turn gives you a national qualification. To find out more about this, take a look at www.auto-route.co.uk.

RAC PROVIDE AUTOMOTIVE SKILLS TRAINING FOR STUDENTS

RAC, one of Britain's leading motoring organisations, have joined together with a school in Nottinghamshire to introduce a pioneering initiative aimed at giving pupils a head start in the automotive industry.

RAC and Ashfield School in Kirkby-in-Ashfield have joined forces to provide students with vocational training that could lead to an Institute of Motor Industry recognised NVQ qualification and an Engineering Diploma. The project is supported by Automotive Skills. Rob Green, Automotive Skills Regional Manager explained: 'This is an excellent example of a recognised employer working in partnership with a forward-thinking school. RAC is working closely with Automotive Skills in developing and then delivering the new Engineering Diploma.'

To help the project, a state-of-the-art vehicle workshop is being built on the school premises, which will be equipped with the latest vehicles and equipment. An RAC automotive engineering trainer will deliver the practical lessons as part of Ashfield School's curriculum. RAC will add further value to the initiative through engaging with local businesses to provide work placements for successful students, as well as providing the opportunity for students to join RAC-supported apprentice programmes.

Damian O'Connor, RAC's Head of Technical Service Delivery said: 'This is a unique and industry-leading initiative where we will combine the Engineering Diploma and Technical Certificate for 14 to 19-year-olds into the existing school curriculum, giving students the opportunity to experience real world training in an adult environment.

'The automotive industry needs to start attracting young people, who would not typically think of joining the motor industry for a career, and who bring a different set of qualities to address the skills gaps now and even more so in the future, particularly in the vehicle diagnosis areas. This programme will look to attract the very best students who will fast-track onto Apprenticeships and continue their technical development at a pace that will help address this concern.

'Master technicians of the future will require a greater understanding of electronics and software programming and as an industry we need to be focused right now on this issue. That is why we have developed this programme with Ashfield School enabling us to build in this level of understanding at an early point in our future technicians' development.'

The lessons will be included in Ashfield School's curriculum from September 2007.

Source: Automotive Skills

However, the usual step is to apply directly for a job in a company in which you are interested – you'll find details of some of these in the Resources section.

COLLEGE STUDENTS AND EMPLOYEES

As already stated, you will most probably be studying one of the Apprenticeship courses, although they have different names in each country for the different levels you may be tackling.

> **DID YOU KNOW?**
>
> There are about 69,000 retail motor businesses in the UK, 84 per cent of which have fewer than ten employees.

When you qualify for your Apprenticeship, you also qualify in Key Skills. Called Core Skills in Scotland, they are not unique to people in the motor industry but are useful to anyone who wants to be successful in any industry or business. There are five Key Skills: Communication, Numeracy, Information technology, Working with others and Problem solving.

The great advantage of Key Skills is that you can take them with you to whatever job you do, whether it's inside or outside the industry, and they will always be of value.

Another benefit is that you also study for a technical certificate while doing an Apprenticeship, or the Scottish equivalent. This means that after you've successfully passed your course, you will have two nationally recognised motor industry qualifications: the NVQ/SVQ and the technical certificate, as well as your more general grounding in Key Skills. You'll find that at the moment the motor industry offers technical certificates in five distinct areas: maintenance and repair, body and paint operations, fitting, parts operations and sales.

When you have successfully achieved your qualifications, you can also apply for a completion certificate, which is issued by Automotive Skills. It may seem that there is quite a lot of paperwork involved in giving you the credentials to show that you've passed your course, but every piece has a good story to tell.

Go to www.automotiveskills.org.uk, the careers website of Automotive Skills for further information. If you want to find out more about Apprenticeships in the retail side of the motor industry, take a look at the IMI website at www.motor.org.uk. If you want to know more about Modern Apprenticeships in Scotland, you should go to www.scottish-enterprise.com.

HOW TO GET A JOB

Perhaps the most effective way of encouraging a company to employ you is if you've done some work for them before.

Apply for work experience while you're still at school if you can and you will be in a terrific position to seek full-time work or an Apprenticeship with the same company

Apply for work experience while you're still at school if you can and, provided there are no disasters during your stint (which might give you valuable knowledge and experience anyway), you will be in a terrific position to seek full-time work or an Apprenticeship with the same company. In terms of training, you will already have shown how keen you are to learn.

You can also gain work experience while studying at college or university. Some companies offer work placements for students in the summer holidays. It's best to contact those you wish to work for directly (there are several manufacturers listed in the Resources section).

WRITING AN EYE-CATCHING CV

Keep it short, no more than two pages, but provide potential employers with the sort of detail that will bring you to their notice. If you haven't yet had many jobs, or even any at all, don't worry. The information to concentrate on is your achievements and the skills you've acquired – and make sure that those skills correspond with ones that any reputable company will be looking for.

Lay out your CV neatly and clearly, regardless of whether you are sending it by post or by email. Check carefully that everything reads well and that there are no mistakes.

WRITING A PUNCHY COVERING LETTER

Compose your covering letter with great care so that it conveys your enthusiasm for joining the company without indulging in overselling. Always create a special letter for each application that addresses what the company is looking for from the ideal candidate. CVs may be standard, but letters must be individual.

For a full examination of how to present yourself on paper, try *Winning CVs for First-Time Job Hunters* by Kathleen Houston (Trotman), which has excellent advice on every stage of the process.

TOP TIPS ON GETTING A JOB

How do you make people offer you work? Here are ten top tips that may help:

- Do some in-depth research on your target company
- Prepare a relevant, customised CV
- Show that you have the energy, commitment and aptitude to work in the industry
- Gain any work experience you can
- Read everything about the industry you can get your hands on
- Apply for training courses at your natural level, e.g. a Modern Apprenticeship
- Snap up any free courses
- Develop other related Key Skills
- Be ready to do anything to gain a start
- Take all the luck you can find (but remember the harder you work, the luckier you get).

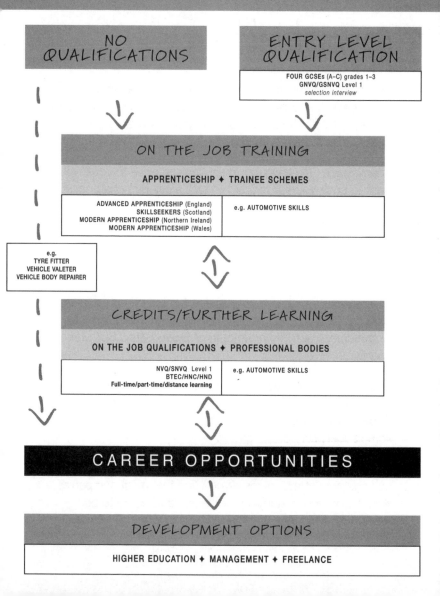

access to

THE MOTOR INDUSTRY

NO QUALIFICATIONS

ENTRY LEVEL QUALIFICATION

FOUR GCSEs (A–C) grades 1–3
GNVQ/GSNVQ Level 1
selection interview

ON THE JOB TRAINING

APPRENTICESHIP ✦ TRAINEE SCHEMES

ADVANCED APPRENTICESHIP (England) SKILLSEEKERS (Scotland) MODERN APPRENTICESHIP (Northern Ireland) MODERN APPRENTICESHIP (Wales)	e.g. AUTOMOTIVE SKILLS

e.g.
**TYRE FITTER
VEHICLE VALETER
VEHICLE BODY REPAIRER**

CREDITS/FURTHER LEARNING

ON THE JOB QUALIFICATIONS ✦ PROFESSIONAL BODIES

NVQ/SNVQ Level 1 BTEC/HNC/HND Full-time/part-time/distance learning	e.g. AUTOMOTIVE SKILLS

CAREER OPPORTUNITIES

DEVELOPMENT OPTIONS

HIGHER EDUCATION ✦ MANAGEMENT ✦ FREELANCE

7

Career opportunities

So, you've got over the first hurdle and found yourself a job, but is it easy to develop your career once you've started in the motor industry? The short answer is yes, if you're willing to work hard and learn both through your studies and on the job.

At any stage, you have four main choices open to you if you want to push yourself forward to tackle different challenges:

- Advance within the company you're working for
- Move to another job in a similar company
- Set up in business on your own
- Transfer to a job outside the industry.

1. The classic path is to advance within the company you're working for. Many people start out by training as a **Vehicle Technician**, **Fast-Fit Technician** or **Body Fitter**. But where do you go from there?

If you want to take the standard route towards the top, your next step would probably be to become a **Workshop Supervisor**. To help you along this path, you'd need to take some supervisory qualifications.

If you wanted further promotion, you could gain some management qualifications – you'll find that most companies will support you in studying for these – and go on to be **Workshop Manager** and then, perhaps, **General Manager**.

Your ultimate goal is to become **Operations Director** or **Managing Director**.

2. What about moving to a different company? Those in sales jobs are often ambitious by nature, so starting as a **Sales Executive** with one company does not mean you will necessarily limit yourself to progressing only within that company. You may have to transfer to another dealership if you want to achieve promotion. Many dealerships will send you on sales, marketing and industry-related courses, so your knowledge will be transferable, but take care to repay such loyalty and investment.

Many dealerships will send you on sales, marketing and industry-related courses, so your knowledge will be transferable

You should only consider moving for absolutely essential reasons. You'll find the best way to progress is to become a **Sales Manager**, often after doing a stint (perhaps on secondment) as **Department Assistant**. You might also usefully spend some time as a **Marketing Manager**.

If you do well in these roles, you can then advance to **Sales Director** and maybe, ultimately, **Managing Director** or **Dealer Principal**.

3. Setting up in business on your own can be risky but it is often a useful progression for those who have provided a specialised service to the industry, such as **Body Fitter**, **Fast-Fit Technician**, **Valeter** or **Specialist Tyre Fitter**.

Your time working for others in the industry will have given you good contacts and enabled you to assess where your future work is likely to come from. But remember that running a business involves a lot more than being good at the technical aspects of the job. You will have to do all your own paperwork and, if you employ others, you will be responsible for wage bills, holiday cover, insurance and many other aspects of business you may not have thought about. However, some of the skills you've developed during your training will really come into their own, such as communicating and dealing with people.

Certain high-powered jobs, such as engineering roles, give you good credentials which can be transferred to other relevant industries

4. Finally, there is always the option of moving outside the industry. Naturally it would be a pity not to continue using all the knowledge you've picked up during your training, but nothing is irreversible. Certain high-powered jobs, such as **engineering** roles, give you good credentials which can be transferred to other relevant industries.

Other jobs, such as **Glazier**, **Trimmer**, **Auto Electrician** or **Mobile Electronics and Security Technician**, provide experience in working with materials and products that attract high demand outside the industry. It might well be possible to set up a business that uses your skills to service a broader market and yet retain some vehicle customers – provided you can get hold of the work space, of course.

This is an industry with real opportunities for advancement. As you go through the training and discover where your strengths lie you will be able to map out a future career path. The diagram below shows options that will open up to you once you have trained.

CAREER OPPORTUNITIES

TRAINING IN KEY MOTOR INDUSTRY SKILLS NVQ LEVEL 1/2

**VEHICLE TECHNICIANS ✦ VEHICLE FITTERS
AUTO ELECTRICIANS ✦ PARTS OPERATIVES**

MORE EXPERIENCE NVQ LEVEL 3 UPWARDS

FINISH APPRENTICESHIPS IN ALL MOTOR INDUSTRY SKILLS AREAS

FURTHER EXPERIENCE NVQ LEVEL 3/4 TRAINING FOR MANAGEMENT

SUPERVISOR/TEAM LEADER ✦ MANAGEMENT SUPPORT

FURTHER EXPERIENCE NVQ LEVEL 4 & 5

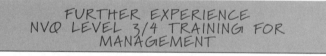

DEPARTMENTAL MANAGER ✦ SALES/MARKETING MANAGEMENT

The last word

8

If you have made it this far through the book, then you should know whether working in the motor industry really is the career for you.

Cars are vital to the British economy and to the smooth passage of our daily lives

Even if you can't yet drive and have never owned a car yourself, you will almost certainly have had daily contact with the automobile. Cars are vital to the British economy and to the smooth passage of our daily lives, and working with them can be an extremely fulfilling experience.

Whatever you want to do in the motor trade, it can be a highly rewarding profession both personally and financially

In fact, the more you think about it, the more you come to realise that the motor industry – and cars in general – are everywhere we look; not just on the roads, but in print advertisements, TV adverts and in a variety of motor sports. Cars even crop up as the 'stars' of films such as *The Italian Job*.

Whether you want to get stuck in under the bonnet and get your hands dirty, or you want to use driving as part of your professional life (as a driving instructor, for example), or if you simply want to match the perfect car to its perfect owner, there is a job in the industry suited to you. You may have dreams of owning a grand prix team, or of designing an award-winning new model, though for most people, more humble ambitions will suffice.

Whatever you want to do in the motor trade, it can be a highly rewarding profession both personally and financially.

If you have made it this far through the book then you should know if the **Motor Industry** really is the career for you. But, before contacting the professional bodies listed in the next chapter, here's a final, fun checklist to show if you have chosen wisely.

THE LAST WORD ✔ TICK YES OR NO

DO YOU LIKE WORKING WITH YOUR HANDS?
☐ YES
☐ NO

DO YOU LIKE WORKING WITH PEOPLE?
☐ YES
☐ NO

DO YOU WANT A JOB WHERE YOU CAN DEVELOP DIFFERENT SKILLS?
☐ YES
☐ NO

ARE YOU SELF-MOTIVATED AND ABLE TO THINK ON YOUR FEET?
☐ YES
☐ NO

ARE YOU ABLE TO COMMUNICATE EFFECTIVELY WITH LOTS OF DIFFERENT PEOPLE?
☐ YES
☐ NO

ARE YOU A SELF-STARTER, ABLE TO TAKE CONTROL AND RESPONSIBILITY?
☐ YES
☐ NO

If you answered 'YES' to all these questions then
CONGRATULATIONS! YOU'VE CHOSEN THE RIGHT CAREER!

If you answered 'NO' to any of these questions then this may not be the career for you.
However, there are still some options open to you.
For example you could work as a Receptionist, Car Sales Person or Garage Assistant.

9

Resources

There are several crucial bodies that you can contact to find out more about following a profession in the motor industry.

Automotive Skills
95 Newman Street
London
W1T 3DT
Free careers helpline: 0800 093 1777
www.automotiveskills.org.uk

Automotive Skills (formerly known as MITC) is the Sector Skills Council for the motor industry. It provides a national focus for training in the industry and is responsible for education training, standards and qualifications. The website offers information about both training courses and qualifications. In conjunction with the *Independent* it publishes the excellent *Career Driven* magazine which is published every six months and goes out to 25,000 secondary schools, universities and colleges. It can also be downloaded from the careers section of the Automotive Skills website. Automotive Skills also produces 'AutoCity', a game-based interactive CD-ROM that acts as a portable careers resource. For copies either order online or call 020 7436 6373.

Institute of the Motor Industry (IMI)
Fanshaws
Brickendon
Hertford

SG13 8PQ
01992 511521
www.motor.org.uk

This is the professional association for individuals employed
in the motor industry and the website contains information
about training and qualifications which include
Apprenticeships and N/SVQs.

VEHICLE MANUFACTURERS
This list of websites for some of the main automobile
manufacturers will be of most use to those wishing to enter
the retail side of the industry.

Audi: www.audi.co.uk
BMW: www.bmw.co.uk
Chrysler: www.chryslerjeep.co.uk
Citroën: www.citroen.co.uk
Fiat: www.fiat.co.uk
Ford: www.ford.co.uk
Honda: www.honda.co.uk
Jaguar: www.jaguarcars.com
Land Rover: www.landrover.com
Mazda: www.mazda.co.uk
Mercedes-Benz: www.mercedes-benz.co.uk
Nissan: www.nissan.co.uk
Peugeot: www.peugeot.co.uk
Porsche: www.porsche.com
Renault: www.renault.co.uk
Saab: www.saab.co.uk
Skoda: www.skoda.co.uk
Toyota: www.toyota.co.uk
Vauxhall: www.vauxhall.co.uk

Volkswagen: www.volkswagen.co.uk
Volvo: www.volvo.com

USEFUL TRAINING ADDRESSES

Listed below are some of the main awarding bodies and general providers of training in the UK:

City & Guilds
1 Giltspur Street
London
EC1A 9DD
020 7294 2800
www.cityandguilds.com

City & Guilds is the leading awarding body for vocational qualifications in the United Kingdom. The excellent website lists all the qualifications it provides which are applicable to the motor industry.

Connexions
www.connexions-direct.com

The Connexions service has been set up especially for those aged 13 to 19 and offers advice, support and practical help on many subjects, including your future career options.

On the Connexions website you will find the jobs4u careers database which you can search for information on training and jobs in the motor trade.

Department for Education and Skills (DfES)
Packs available by calling 0800 585505
www.dfes.gov.uk

If you are undertaking a vocational training course lasting up to two years (including one year's practical work experience if it is part of the course), you may be eligible for a Career Development Loan (see www.lifelonglearning.co.uk for more info). These are available for full-time, part-time and distance learning courses and applicants can be employed, self-employed or unemployed. The DfES pays interest on the loan for the length of the course and up to one month afterwards.

Department of Trade and Industry (DTI)
www.autoindustry.co.uk/education/careers

This website offers advice and information on getting into the industry.

Edexcel
One90 High Holborn
London
WC1V 7BH
0870 240 9800
www.edexcel.org.uk

Edexcel has taken over from BTEC in offering BTEC qualifications, including Higher National Certificates (HNCs) and Higher National Diplomas (HNDs). It also offers NVQ qualifications. The website includes qualification 'quick links' and you can search either by qualification or by the career in which you are interested.

EMTEC
0115 846 1200
www.emtec-training.co.uk/index2.htm

SORT IT OUT!

HOW DO I KNOW WHICH JOBS ARE RIGHT FOR ME?

No problem, you can log onto **cityandguilds.com/myperfectjob** and take 20 minutes to answer a range of online questions which looks at your interests, personality and lifestyle and suggests job areas which may suit you. Get all the information on job options, how to get started and where you can go to study.
cityandguilds.com/myperfectjob

The Suzuki Advanced Modern Apprenticeship is run by EMTEC, which is part of the Carter & Carter Group. It is based in Nottingham and runs courses for Suzuki and most of the major manufacturers in the motor and motorcycle trades.

Learning and Skills Council
Cheylesmore House
Quinton Road
Coventry
CV1 2WT
0845 019 4170
Apprenticeship helpline: 0800 015 0600
www.lsc.gov.uk
www.apprenticeships.org.uk

Launched in 2001, Learning and Skills Council now has a main office in Coventry and nine regional offices. It is responsible for the largest investment in post-16 education and training in England and this includes further education colleges, work-based training and workforce developments. For 2006/7 its budget is £10.4 billion.

In Scotland:
www.modernapprenticeships.com
www.careers.scotland.org.uk

In Wales:
www.beskilled.net
www.careerswales.com

New Deal
0845 606 2626
www.newdeal.co.uk

If you are an older individual looking to change career and you have been unemployed for six months or more (or are receiving Jobseeker's Allowance), you may be able to gain access to NVQ/SVQ courses through the New Deal programme. People with disabilities, ex-offenders and lone parents are eligible before reaching six months of unemployment. Check the website for more information. New Deal is part of the Department for Work and Pensions.

Qualifications and Curriculum Authority (QCA)
83 Piccadilly
London
W1J 8QA
020 7509 5555
www.qca.org.uk

In Scotland:
Scottish Qualifications Authority (SQA)
Optima Building
58 Robertson Street
Glasgow
G2 8DQ
Customer contact centre: 0141 242 2214
www.sqa.org.uk

These official awards bodies will be able to tell you whether the course you choose leads to a nationally approved qualification such as NVQ or SVQ.

PUBLICATIONS

Automotive News Europe
www.europe.autonews.com

This weekly publication contains news features on the
industry throughout Europe.

Autotimes
Lloyds Bank Chambers
34 High Street
Marsh
PE15 9JR
01354 656555
www.autotimes.co.uk

This monthly magazine covers parts and equipment
purchasing for garages, bodyshops and retail accessory
shops.

Car Mechanics
Cudham Tithe Barn
Berry's Hill
Cudham
TN16 3AG
01959 541444
www.carmechanicsmag.co.uk

This monthly magazine covers servicing, repairs and major
accident damage.

Driving Instructor
Safety House
Beddington Farm Road
Croydon
CR0 4XZ
020 8665 5151
www.driving.org

There are six issues of this magazine a year, covering developments in the world of driving instruction. It is published by the Driving Instructors Association.

Tyre Trade News
6B Acorn Farm Business Centre
Cublington Road
Wing
LU7 OLB
01296 681424
www.tyretradenews.co.uk

This monthly magazine carries product news and information for the tyre trade.